# Anna Jarvis and the Story of Mother's Day

written and illustrated by E.Hefferin

Dedicated to my mother
Veronica Brunner Hefferin
with gratitude for her love and inspiration.

Special thanks to
Olive Dadisman
and to my sister
Teresa.

Anna Jarvis was born May 1, 1864 in the house her father had built. The house, which is in Webster, West Virginia, is now a museum that visitors can tour.

The railroad ran across the street from the Jarvis home, and from their house, Anna's family could see and hear the trains.

Anna was inspired by her mother, who helped people by starting the Mother's Day Work Clubs. Anna's uncle, who was a doctor, helped the clubs teach healthy things such as boiling milk before drinking it.

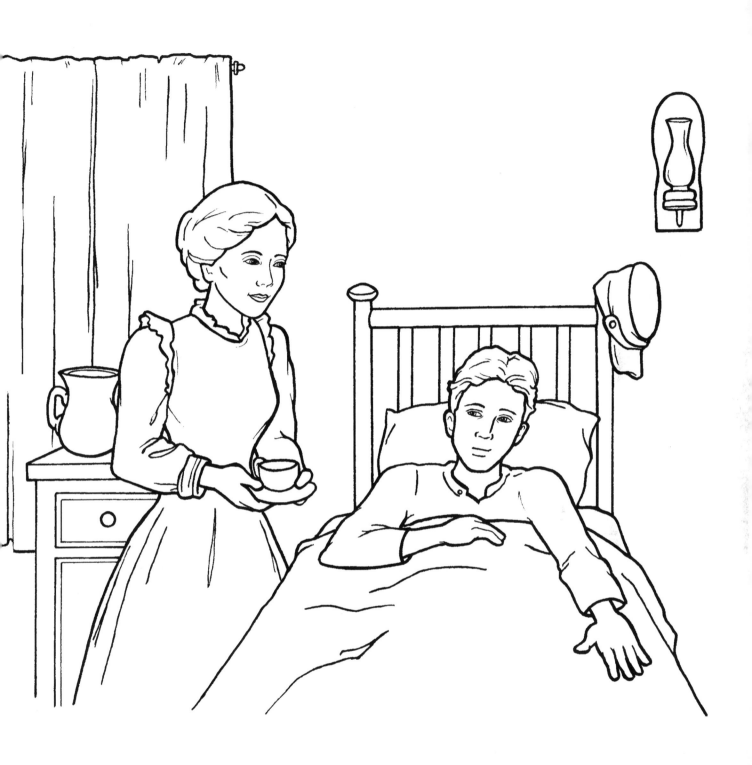

During the Civil War, Anna's mother provided care
for soldiers who were sick or injured.

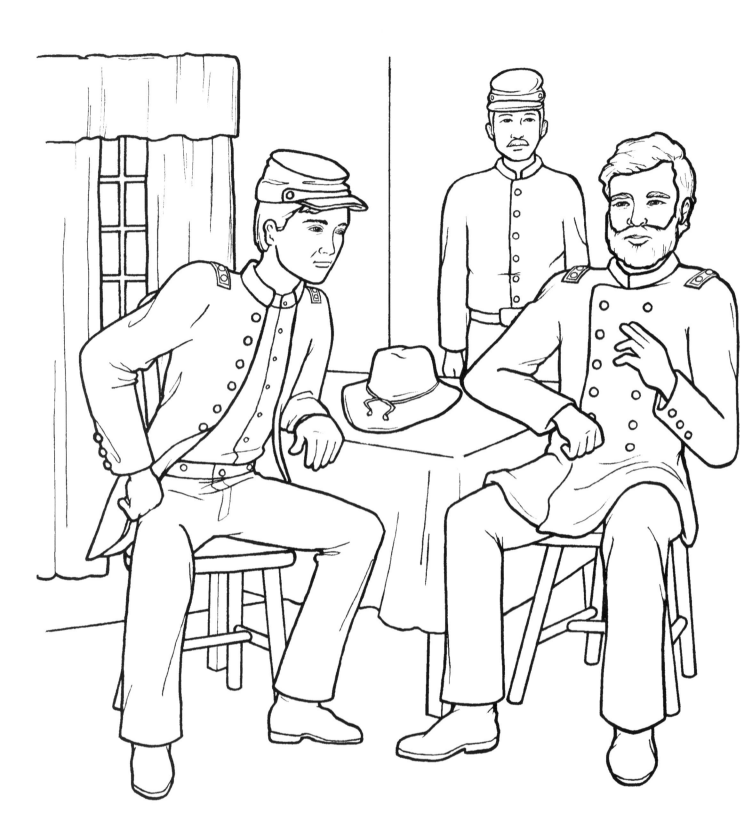

Anna was born during the Civil War. Military officers, including General George McClellan, used her family's home for meetings.

Anna's brother Josiah was so happy to have his little sister in the family that he carved her initials in the fireplace mantle, and they are still there.

After the Civil War, Anna's mother organized Mother's Friendship Day, an annual event that brought together soldiers, families and neighbors from both sides of the war.

Anna's mother could play the piano, and Anna learned to play it, too. Anna could also play the violin.

Anna's father was a minister, and her mother taught Sunday school. When Anna was twelve, she heard her mother say a prayer that someone would someday create a special day to honor mothers.

In 1896, Anna moved to Philadelphia to live with her brother Claude. Her mother and her sister, Lillie, also came there to live with them after Anna's father died in 1902.

At her mother's death in 1905, Anna made a promise to establish the day to honor mothers that her mother had hoped for. She wrote many letters to important people asking for their help and gave public speeches in her efforts to create Mother's Day.

John Wanamaker, a successful businessman in Philadelphia, provided Anna with much support and assistance in her campaign to create Mother's Day.

A service was held to honor mothers in the Jarvis' former
church in Grafton, West Virginia on May 12, 1907.

On May 10, 1908, the first official Mother's Day service was held at the same church, Andrews M. E. Church, which is now the International Mother's Day Shrine. Anna sent 500 white carnations from Philadelphia to be given to the mothers attending the service.

Also, in the afternoon on May 10, 1908, Anna was the guest speaker at a Mother's Day service that was organized by John Wanamaker and held in Philadelphia.

# Fill in the missing word in each sentence:

Anna was __ o __ __ in the house her father built.

Anna's last name was __ a __ __ __ __.

She could __ __ __ y the piano and the violin.

Mother's Day is always on the second Sunday in M __ __.

Anna's mother started the Mother's Day __ __ r __ Clubs.

Her mother also cared for sick s __ __ __ __ __ __ __
during the Civil War.

Anna worked as a t __ __ __ __ __ __ after she finished
college.

Anna moved to __ h __ __ __ __ __ __ __ __ __ __
to live with her brother.

She wrote many __ e __ __ __ __ __ asking for help in
creating Mother's Day.

Mother's Friendship D __ __ was a celebration that brought
together people from both sides of the Civil War.

# Unscramble the letters in the boxes and write them here:

__ __ __ __ __ __ __ ' __ __ __

In 1909, Mother's Day services were held in 45 states and in Hawaii, Puerto Rico, Canada and Mexico.

Anna Jarvis lived in West Virginia and Pennsylvania. If you can find these states, write her initials, A.J., in them. If you live in the United States, put your initials in any states where you have lived.

In 1914, President Woodrow Wilson signed a resolution designating Mother's Day to be celebrated on the second Sunday of May every year.

```
R  H  E  L  P  C  Q  U  X  C
J  Z  R  O  X  A  B  L  H  A
A  K  A  V  Y  R  F  E  B  M
R  E  C  E  F  N  Z  T  Q  P
V  S  S  K  N  A  H  T  J  A
I  I  Q  M  O  T  H  E  R  I
S  M  A  Y  B  I  X  R  B  G
H  O  N  O  R  O  F  S  J  N
Q  R  Z  S  U  N  D  A  Y  T
S  P  E  E  C  H  E  S  P  K
```

## Can you find these words?

| | | | |
|---|---|---|---|
| campaign | honor | May | Sunday |
| care | Jarvis | mother | thanks |
| carnation | letters | promise | |
| help | love | speeches | |

Many people treat their mothers, or someone else who has cared for them, in a special way on Mother's Day. They show their love and appreciation by giving her cards, gifts or flowers, or by doing some nice thing for her.

Made in the USA
Charleston, SC
20 August 2011